WHERE IS BABY K?

K. S. Daniels   A. Muriasova

This book is dedicated
to my darling daughter
Keonni Selah Daniels-Davis.

Mommy K will celebrate today.

For Baby K is days away.

She dances with friends and joy fills the air.

While swinging her dress and tossing her hair.

Shenzhen 深圳

Baby K enjoys a stroll with Mommy.
The beauty in the park makes her feel
cozy like the tummy.
Today she sleeps and dreams of
cheerful sounds.
People are singing and twisting on the
grounds.

Baby K travels to a great place today.

She left China to visit the USA.

Together, with Mommy, they walk to city hall.

They see memorable sites, some big and some small.

Baby K is exploring the City of Love.

She looks at the skyline and moon up above.

The family eats a famous and yummy water ice.

Today is amazing and full of delights.

Baby K travels a bit south to see the capital of the country, Washington DC. There are grand landmarks from times of the past.

For now, they thrive in the present as time moves fast.

Another trip, another flight.

So where is Baby K roaming tonight?

After flying on planes, she is back home in the Far East.

Perhaps she will nap as her journeys cease.

No, absolutely not! Baby K's travels never dwindle.

She takes a taxi to a marvelous temple.

The scenery is peaceful, beautiful, and exciting.

"Where to next Mommy?" ... "Only time will tell darling."

Baby K loves going on adventures and trips.

She has traveled on planes, trains, cars and small ships.

Today she rides the metro as she plots her next move

To explore the globe forever, not just in her youth.

K. S. Daniels is the author of the children's book, Where Is Baby K? She is a multifaceted international educator who has taught children of all ages both in the USA and in China. She has a profound passion for traveling and for teaching the Spanish language. She is a graduate of Temple University and resides in the USA.

Anastasiya Muriasova is the illustrator of dozens of books for children. Mother by day and kids' artist by nights. Coming from Russia and currently living in Shanghai, she is an amateur artist with great passion to watercolor.